RESOURCE GUIDE
SING ALONG & READ ALONG WITH Dr. JEAN

Written by
Dr. Jean Feldman
and
Dr. Holly Karapetkova

Editor:	Dorothy Ly
Illustrator:	Darcy Tom
Designer/Production:	Andrew Choo
Art Director:	Moonhee Pak
Project Director:	Stacey Faulkner

Table of Contents

Introduction

Why

Teach along with Dr. Jean! This valuable resource guide is full of fun and lively classroom activities designed to accompany the *Sing Along & Read Along with Dr. Jean* collection. The cross-curricular activities provide opportunities for the teacher to enhance the learning concepts that are introduced and explored in each book and song. The ideas relate to curriculum areas such as reading, writing, math, science and social studies. The user-friendly standards chart will help connect each book to early childhood standards.

For each of the 12 books in the *Sing Along & Read Along with Dr. Jean* series, you'll find
- Three to four activities that extend the theme and featured learning concept.
- Two reproducible pages directly related to the activities.
- Several additional short and simple activity suggestions.

The National Institute for Literacy has identified five areas of reading instruction: phonemic awareness, phonics, fluency, vocabulary, and text comprehension. Motivation and engagement, oral language, and writing are essential to reading success. The activities suggested in this book clearly support these reading competencies.

Research by the National Early Literacy Panel suggests certain skills and abilities have direct links to early literacy success. Young children need engaging, hands-on opportunities with alphabet knowledge, print knowledge, and oral language. The magic of this book is that it will nurture these skills in such a fun way that children won't even realize they are learning!

Ten Reasons to Sing Along and Read Along!

1. Music is multisensory. The more senses you use to reach the brain, the more likely the message will get there.

2. If children are exposed to concepts while singing, they will learn those concepts more easily when they are formally introduced.

3. Music nurtures phonological awareness such as alliteration and rhyme.

4. Music activates the brain. It can be used as an "indicator" to help children know what to expect. It can also energize learning.

5. Songs and chants are a natural way to develop oral language, auditory memory, and fluency.

6. Poems and songs lay a foundation for common knowledge in the classroom.

7. Children are able to use their imagination and create pictures in their brains when they sing. This is an important part of reading comprehension.

8. Repetition is a key to learning. Children will enjoy singing these songs over and over again.

9. Singing and dancing relieve stress and oxygenate the brain.

10. Through music and movement, all children can feel successful. A "community of learners" is enhanced when teachers and children enjoy something together!

Remember: What matters most is the spirit and enthusiasm you share, not your voice. Children don't know if you can't sing, so just open your mouth and make a happy sound!

Ways to Use the *Sing Along & Read Along* Books

Why

It's important to model the joy of reading every day in your classroom. Use the *Sing Along & Read Along* books for large group experiences, small group instruction, and individual student use.

What

SHARED READING

Introduce the books one at a time during circle time or story time. Singing and reading the books several times will support children's fluency. Choose a book that supports a particular theme, concept, or skill presented in class. Point out letters, words, or punctuation or call children's attention to the details in the pictures and discuss the characters or story setting.

SUGGESTIONS

Independent Reading

Make the books available to the children in the classroom library so they can visit them over and over. Place the books in a special basket or tub labeled *Sing Along & Read Along with Dr. Jean.*

Partner Reading

Let children look at books with a partner. Invite them to sing songs independently or picture read.

Graphing

After introducing all of the books, make a graph of children's favorites.

LISTENING CENTER

Make tapes of songs to use at your listening center. It might be helpful to record each song three times as repetition increases children's confidence and skills.

MUSICAL BOOKS

Place a chair for each child in a circle. Put a *Sing Along & Read Along* book or other classroom book in each chair. Play a song and have children march around the chairs. When the music stops, have children sit in the chair nearest to them. Ask each child to look at the book in his or her chair for about one minute. Then ask several children questions about their books: *What is your book about? Who is a character in your book?* or *What is the setting?* After you have asked your questions, instruct children to replace the books in their chairs, stand, and begin marching again to the music. Repeat this several times to pique children's interest in books.

Point and Read

Reading pointers are a helpful tool for children to use to track print as they sing or read. The pointers will help children make the connection between the spoken word and written word, and they will help develop eye-hand coordination and left-to-right orientation.

Eye Can Read!

Have each child glue a wiggly eye to the end of a jumbo craft stick. Remind children to keep their "eyes" on the words as they sing or read.

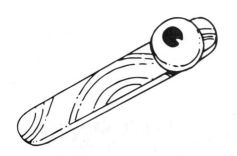

Magic Wand

Give each child a chopstick. Let him or her dip one end in glue and then dip it in glitter. Allow chopsticks to dry overnight. Have children use these "magic wands" to identify letters and words they can read in the books.

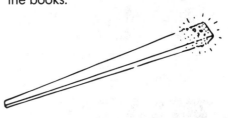

Theme Pointer

Take a craft stick or straw and add stickers or fun foam shapes that relate to the songs. For example, a glow-in-the-dark star for *Twinkle Friends*, or a monkey sticker for tracking text in *Five Little Monkeys*.

Invisible Paintbrush

Give children small, clean paintbrushes, and encourage them to find and "paint" details on each page. Guide students with questions such as *Can you find the blueberries? Where is the spider? What number did the old lady eat on this page?*

Standards

The National Association for the Education of Young Children has identified a number of concepts and skills that are important to children's learning and development. Below are some examples of how the *Sing Along & Read Along* books can support early childhood standards.

Social/Emotional Development

As children sing along with these books, they will learn how to cooperate and be a part of a social group. *Twinkle Friends* and *May There Always Be Sunshine* support feelings of worthiness and a sensitivity toward others.

Physical Development

As children make hand motions and actions for these songs, and do the related activities, they will be developing both large and small motor skills as well as improving rhythmic skills. *Dinosaur Boogie* and *Action Alphabet* will enhance large motor skills.

Language Development

The songs presented in this series of books are ones that children will beg to sing again and again. In addition to enhancing oral language development, the books provide a bridge for print knowledge. The activities for *My Mother Is a Baker* and *Rules Rap* will expand children's background knowledge and vocabulary development.

Early Literacy

Nursery Rhyme Rally and *Color Train* offer a natural way to play with rhymes and words. *Action Alphabet* supports early literacy skills such as learning letter names and phonemic awareness. Children will experience other concepts about books, comprehension, and writing with the extension activities for each story.

Early Mathematics

Five Little Monkeys and *I Know an Old Lady Who Swallowed a One* will help children learn numerals, number words, and counting forwards and backwards. *My Mother Is a Baker* and *My Hands on My Head* introduce students to repetition and patterns.

Science

Use *My Mother Is a Baker* as a springboard for talking about the five senses and health. *Birdies* enables children to explore the concept of mother and baby animals, and *Dinosaur Boogie* offers opportunities for discussing habitats and animal characteristics.

Social Studies

Fairness, friendship, and diversity are reinforced with *Rules Rap* and *My Hands on My Head*. *My Mother Is a Baker* is perfect for talking about families and occupations.

Creative Expression and the Arts

The extension activities for each of the books provide numerous possibilities for children to explore drama, art, and music.

| | STANDARDS | | | | | | | |
TITLE	Social/Emotional Development	Physical Development	Language Development	Early Literacy	Early Mathematics	Science	Social Studies	Creative Expression and the Arts
Color Train			●	●				
Five Little Monkeys				●	●			●
Action Alphabet		●		●				●
Dinosaur Boogie		●		●		●		●
Rules Rap	●		●	●			●	●
Birdies				●		●		●
Nursery Rhyme Rally			●	●				●
May There Always Be Sunshine	●			●				●
I Know an Old Lady Who Swallowed a One				●	●			
Twinkle Friends	●			●			●	●
My Mother Is a Baker			●	●	●	●	●	●
My Hands on My Head			●	●	●		●	

Chug-Around-the-Rug

Have children line up behind each other. Demonstrate how to place your hands on the person's shoulders in front of you to form a train. Identify the first child as the engineer and the last child as the caboose, and invite the children to chug around the room to the song.

Colorful Show–and–Tell

Give each child a brown paper lunch bag and ask him or her to take it home and bring back something that is the child's favorite color. Ask parents to write three clues about the object on the bag. Assist the child in reading the clues to classmates as they play "detective" and try to figure out what is in the bag.

Color Train

Why

This book reinforces color recognition, rhyme, and the concept that letters put together make words.

What

COLOR WORD PUZZLES

Write color words on sentence strips or colored paper to make word puzzles. Cut between the letters of each word, and place the pieces in an envelope. Write the color word on the front so the children have a model to follow as they put the color word puzzle together.

COLOR BRACELETS

Have children use pipe cleaners and colored beads to make a bracelet to go along with the story. First make a list on chart paper of the colors in the order in which they appear in the book. Write each word with the appropriate color of crayon to support children in reading the words. (You will have to use white crayon on black paper for white.) Next, model how to line the beads up in the correct order. Then show children how to string the beads one at a time onto the pipe cleaner. Help children twist the ends to make a bracelet. Have children sing the song, touching the beads as each color is named.

COLOR WHIZ

Teach your students about primary and secondary colors with this simple experiment. You will need six clear plastic cups; water; red, blue, and yellow food coloring; and an overhead projector. Arrange the cups in a circle similar to the example below. Fill every other cup halfway with water (three cups total). Then add the food coloring to the cups with water: red to one, blue to the next, and yellow to the last. Pour a little of the red water and a little of the blue water into the empty cup between those colors. Voila! Purple! Repeat to make orange (red and yellow) and green (yellow and blue). Explain that red, yellow, and blue are primary colors and they can be mixed to form the secondary colors purple, orange, and green.

After you have demonstrated Color Whiz, have children do their own experiments. Give them eyedroppers, coffee filters, and cups of red, blue, and yellow water colored with food coloring. Ask them to put two drops of different colors together on a coffee filter and observe the results. Have students record their discoveries on the reproducible on page 10.

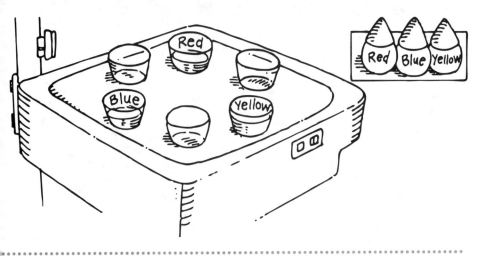

COLORFUL TRAIN

Use the patterns on page 11 to make colorful train books. Copy a class set on white card stock. Invite children to color the train engine and caboose and cut them out. Give each child 10 index cards to make the "train cars." Have children write the name of each color in *Color Train* on the cars in black marker. Then have them use crayon or colored pencil to color the index cards with the matching color. Or ask children to use corresponding colored markers to write the color words and then draw pictures of objects that represent the colors. Assist children in hole-punching the train engine, caboose, and index cards to connect them end-to-end using yarn, string, or small plastic book rings. Show children how to fold the book closed accordion style. As you sing or read *Color Train* together, have children unfold each train car and reveal the colorful trains.

Transition Time

Use this song as a transition when children move to centers, line up, or wash their hands. Ask, *What color are you wearing today? When you hear that color in the song, you may stand up and go to a center (or get your lunchbox, etc.).*

Picture This

Read through the book slowly, displaying one page at a time. Tell the children to use their eyes to find the objects that they hear as you read. Invite different children to come up and touch the various objects with a finger or a pointer.

Name _____ Date _____

Color Whiz

Directions: Color the first two circles to match the two colors you mixed. Color the last circle to show what you discovered about mixing these colors.

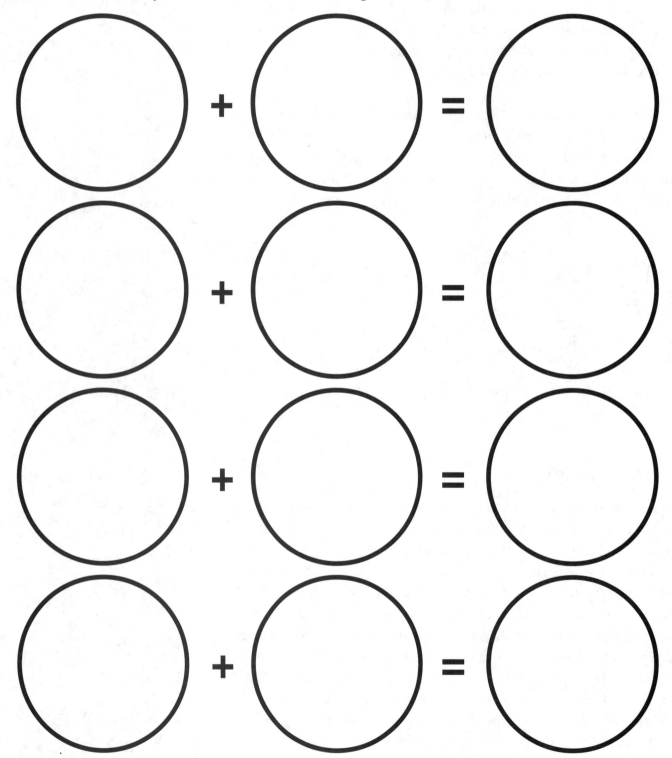

Sing Along & Read Along with Dr. Jean Resource Guide © 2008 Creative Teaching Press

Colorful Train

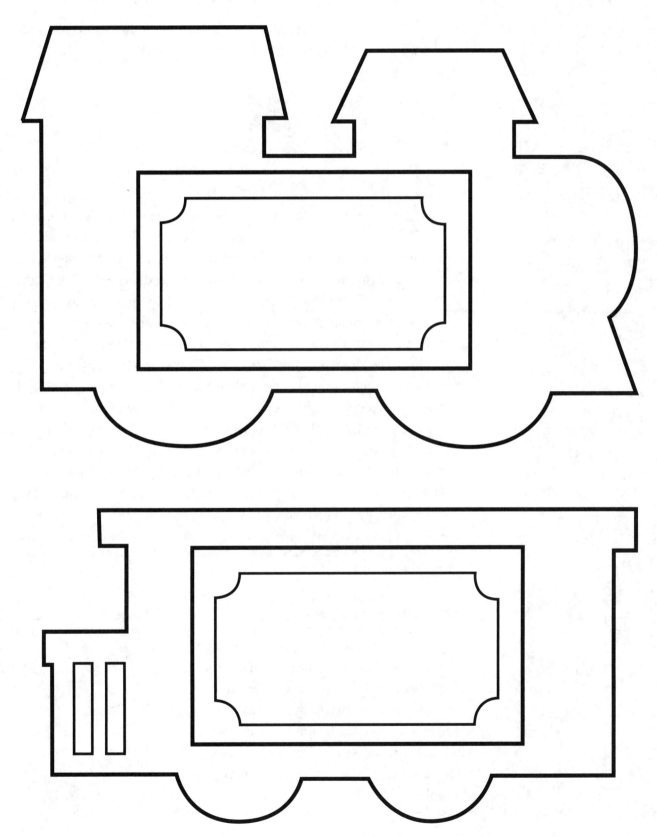

Five Little Monkeys

Real and Pretend

Check out some books from the library with pictures of real monkeys. Compare the pictures of real monkeys with those in *Five Little Monkeys*. Ask children to think about how the monkeys are alike and how they are different.

Forwards and Backwards

Choose different groups of children to come to the front of the room to be monkeys. Demonstrate how to count the "monkeys" forwards. Then stop and say, *Now, let's see if we can count backwards.* Continue making other sets of monkeys (from one to ten) in the front of the room. Invite different children to come up and count their friends forwards and then backwards.

Why

This book reinforces numeral and number word recognition, counting backwards, and the concept of subtraction.

What

ACT IT OUT!

Make five copies of the reproducible patterns on page 14. Color and cut out the ears and snouts. To make monkey ear headbands, glue the ears to the center of sentence strips (or 2" x 22" strips of paper). To make alligator headbands, fold along the dotted lines. Glue the tabs to the front center of a sentence strip at an angle to make the snout stand up like a tent. Cut two oval-shaped eyes from white construction paper and use a marker to draw circles for eyeballs. Glue the eyes above the alligator snout. Choose six volunteers to play the parts of the five monkeys and the alligator. Fit all of the headband strips to the children's heads and staple. Have the monkeys stand on one side of the room and the alligator stand on the other side of the room. As the class sings along with the book, let the alligator choose one monkey each time and pretend to snap at him or her. Instruct monkeys to sit on the floor after the alligator has snapped at them. Then at the end, have all the monkeys jump up and say, "Missed me! Missed me! Now you've got to kiss me!"

Hint! Invite four volunteers in the audience to wear the remaining alligator headbands and participate by imitating the alligator by sticking out their arms to open and shut them like the alligator's mouth.

MONKEYS IN A TREE

Copy the reproducible on page 15 for each child. Have children color and cut out the the treetop with the monkeys in the tree and the tree trunk. Help children attach the monkey section behind the trunk with a brass fastener. As children sing the song, invite them to turn the wheel and make the monkeys disappear.

Hint! Enlarge the reproducible to 154.5% (5½ x 8½ ◄8½ x 14) to give little hands more room to work.

ALLIGATOR GAME

You will need an empty can from icing or powered drink mix and 13 jumbo craft sticks to make this game. Cover the can with green construction paper and draw big eyes as shown below. Write the numbers 0–10 on the ends of 11 of the craft sticks. Photocopy the two alligator images from this page. Then color, and cut out the images, and glue them to the ends of the last two sticks. Mix up the sticks and insert them in the can with the numbers and alligators toward the bottom. Say this chant to begin the game:

> **There's a big, hungry alligator sneaking up on you, and he's going to take a bite if you don't know what to do. So open up your ears and do what I say. Are you ready? Get set! Let's play!**

Pass the can to the first child. Have him or her pull a stick from the can, identify the number, return the stick to the can and then pass the can to the next child. If a child doesn't know the number, encourage him or her to "phone a friend" (ask a classmate) for help. Have any child who draws an alligator from the can, jump up and open and close his or her arms like the mouth of the alligator. Continue the game until each child has had a turn.

Hint! Adapt the number of sticks to the ability of your students. You could also put letters, colors, or words on the sticks.

Monkey Math

Encourage children to count the monkeys on each page in the book. Remind them to touch each monkey as they count it. Have children sing along with the song, and encourage them to hold up fingers for the number of monkeys on each page.

Inequalities

Use sets of students to demonstrate inequalities. Make a set with two children and a set with four children. Explain that you are an alligator and that you are very hungry! Ask, *Which set would I like to eat?* Open up your hands and pretend to eat the set of four. Draw the following on the board: 2 < 4. Say, *Two is less than four* as you point to the symbols. Do similar demonstrations, encouraging the children to make their arms like the alligator as you ask, *Which set would you like to eat? Why?*

Monkey and Alligator Headbands

Monkey Ears

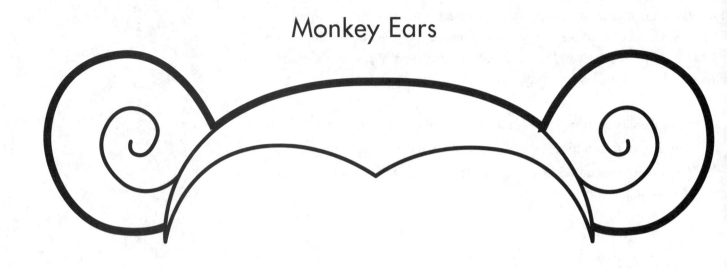

Alligator Snout

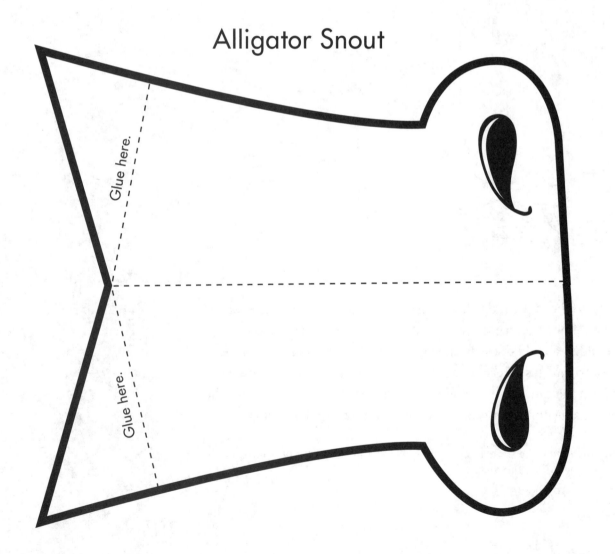

Glue here.

Glue here.

Monkeys in a Tree

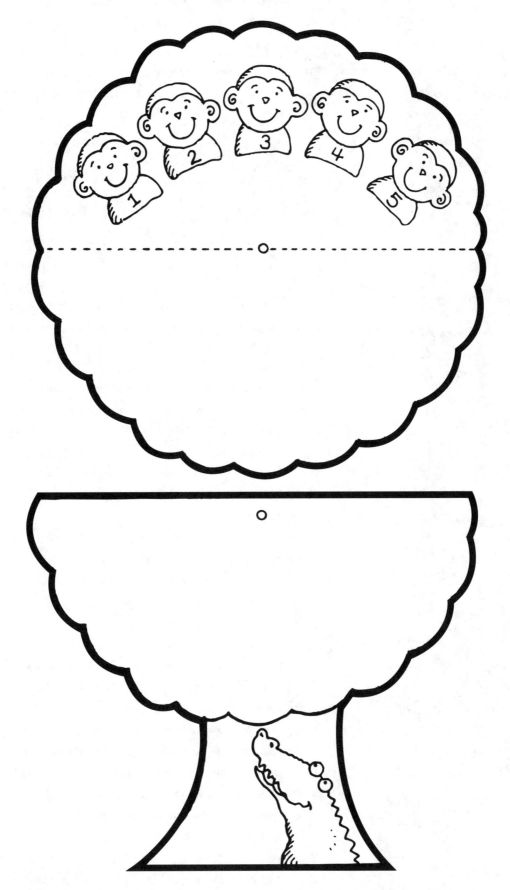

Action Alphabet

Why Children need many experiences in playing with letters and sounds before they are ready to read. This book provides a meaningful way to introduce the alphabet.

A for apple

P-P-P-Pop a Word

Use alliteration with each letter and encourage children to "pop" out words that start the same. For example: "/a/ /a/ /a/ apple, Annie, anteater," or "/b/ /b/ /b/ bounce, ball, baby, book, bubble."

Letter Sticks

Glue foam letters to jumbo craft sticks. Pass these out to the children, and then have them come up one at a time and match their letters to the corresponding letters in the book. Invite them to walk around the room and match their letters to other letters in the room.

What

LETTER DANCE

Have children stand and make motions for each letter as it is sung in the song. Suggestions for movements have been provide below.

A for **apple**–hold up a fist and pretend to eat

B for **bounce**–bounce an invisible ball

C for **cut**–open and close middle and index finger

D for **dig**–pretend to hold a shovel and dig

E for **elbow**–stick out elbows

F for **fan**–use hand like a fan

G for **gallop**–pretend to hold reins and gallop

H for **hop**–stand on one foot and hop

I for **itch**–scratch sides

J for **jump**–jump on both feet

K for **kick**–gently kick one foot

L for **love**–wrap arms around self and hug

M for **munch**–chew with lips together

N for **nod**–shake head up and down

O for **opera**–extend arms as you sing

P for **push**–take palms and pretend to push in front of you

Q for **quiet**–put index finger over lips

R for **run**–run in place

S for **sew**–take index finger and thumb and pretend to sew

T for **talk**–hold up hands and open and close thumbs to fingers

U for **upside down**–lean head over and look through legs

V for **volley**–palms up in air as if hitting a ball

W for **wiggle**–wiggle body all around

X for **x-ray**–cross arms in front of you like an "x"

Y for **yawn**–place hand over mouth and pretend to yawn

Z for **zigzag**–make a giant "z" in front of you with your index finger

SENSORY LETTERS

Use a water-soluble marker to make dotted letters. Put drops of glue on the top of the dots. When the glue dries, have children trace over the dots with their fingers and "feel" the letters. Make additional letters from sandpaper, felt, and other textures to give children sensory experiences.

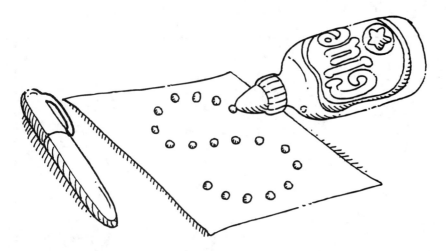

SIGN LANGUAGE

Sign language is a powerful way to get information to the brain because it is multisensory. As you sing this song, model how to make the sign for each letter using the illustrations on page 18. Teach each child the manual sign for the first letter in his or her name. Sing children's names to the tune of "If You're Happy and You Know It."

 If your name is Kyle, your sign is (make sign for K).
If your name is Mimi, your sign is (make sign for M).
If your name is José, your sign is (make sign for J).
If your name is Amy, your sign is (make sign for A).
If your name is Ruben, your sign is (make sign for R).

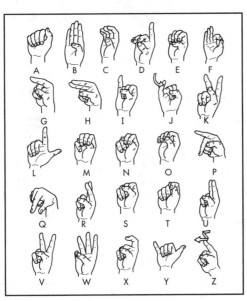

Name Poem

Use the reproducible on page 19 to introduce children to acrostic poetry. Have children use the letters of their first names and fill in the lines with words or phrases that begin with each letter to create a fun poem. Invite children to share their poems with a partner or the whole class.

Alphabet Art

Use a marker to write each letter of the alphabet in large print on separate sheets of paper. Let each child choose a letter and try to create a picture out of the letter. Put the pictures together to make a class book.

Class ABC Book

Let each child choose a word from the book and act it out. Take digital photos of the children making the motions, and then put the photos together to make a class book.

Name _____   Date _____

Finger Spelling Alphabet

Directions: Use the following signs to spell out names of people and places.

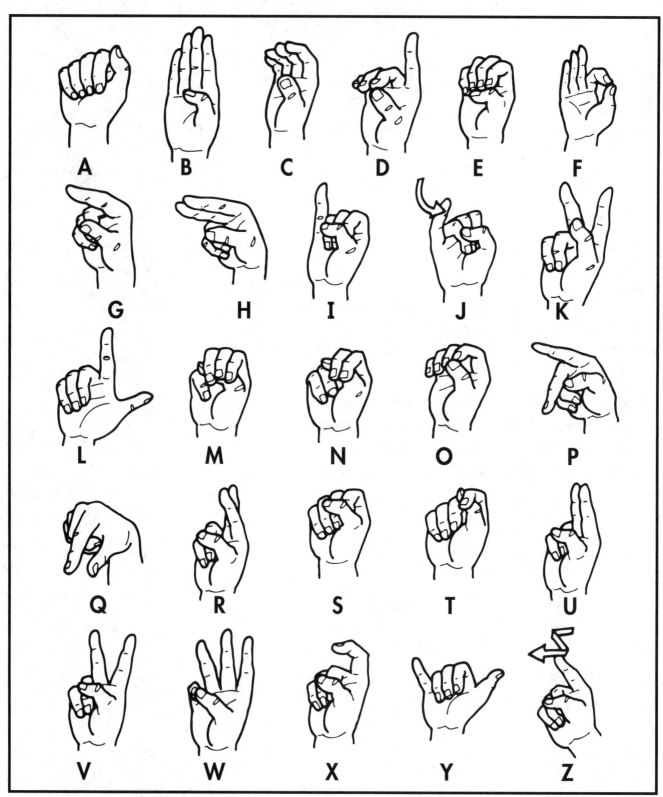

Sing Along & Read Along with Dr. Jean Resource Guide © 2008 Creative Teaching Press

Name Poem

Write each of the letters of your first name in the following boxes and complete the sentences.

☐ is for _____.

☐ is for _____.

☐ is for _____.

☐ is for _____.

☐ is for _____.

☐ is for _____.

☐ is for _____.

☐ is for _____.

☐ is for _____.

Paleontologists

Explain what fossils are and what paleontologists do. Get plastic dinosaurs and mold egg shapes around them with play dough. Then have children use craft sticks and toothpicks to dig out the dinosaurs.

Dino Habitats

Have children look at the pictures in the book and describe the dinosaurs' habitat. Give them paper, and ask them to draw the dinosaurs' habitat. Allow children to use pictures from the memory game (page 23) to glue dinosaurs on the habitat, or have them draw their own pictures of dinosaurs.

Dinosaur Boogie

Why

This book is an excellent springboard for vocabulary and science, offering opportunities for discussions about habitats and animal characteristics. It's also a good way for children to practice determining facts from looking at pictures.

What

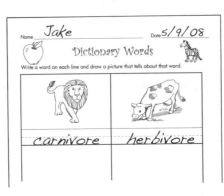

DICTIONARY WORDS

After reading the story, look through the book and ask children about the words they might not be familiar with, such as *carnivore* and *herbivore*. Brainstorm with your students what they can do if they don't know the meaning of a word. Ideas might include asking a parent or a friend or looking on the Internet. Suggest looking up words in the dictionary if children do not think of it. Get a dictionary and model looking up words from the book. Explain to the children that whenever they hear a word they don't understand, they should say, *That's a dictionary word! Let's look it up.* Provide a copy of the reproducible on page 22 for each student to record words he or she is unfamiliar with. Keep a language experience chart of words children discover naturally as you read and sing.

Memory Game

Use the dinosaur cards on page 23 to make a memory game for the children to play. Ask children to cut out all of the cards. Have children place the cards facedown on the floor.

Then invite children to turn over two cards at a time and try to match the ones that go together. After children have played the game at school, send it home for them to play with their families.

DINOSAUR DANCE ALONG

Teach children the following motions so they can dance along with the dinosaurs!

Pterosaurs had wings and could fly.
(Stretch out arms and flap them up and down.)

Tyrannosaurus Rex, king of the swamp.
(Open and close arms like a giant mouth.)

Do the dinosaur boogie, start bouncing around.
(Bounce up and down.)

Hands like claws make a growling sound–Grrr!
(Make hands like claws and growl.)

Stomp, stomp, stomp the ground.
(Stomp feet.)

Then wiggle and turn around.
(Raise hands in the air, dance, and turn around.)

Brontosaurus was the largest of all.
(Stand on tip toes and pretend to grab leaves and put them in your mouth.)

Triceratops had three horns on his head.
(Stick up three fingers and put them on top of your head.)

Dino Research

Brainstorm with the class questions they have about dinosaurs. Together do an Internet search to look for facts about dinosaurs or visit your school library and check out books about dinosaurs. After reading some of the books to the children, ask them to share facts they learned. Record their ideas on chart paper.

Picture Reading

Focus on the illustrations in the book by looking at one dinosaur picture at a time. Ask questions such as *What can you tell me about a pterosaur by looking at the picture? What else can you tell me? What did Tyrannosaurus Rex do? What else can you tell me about it?*

Name _____ Date _____

Dictionary Words

Write a word on each line and draw a picture that tells about that word.

Dinosaur Memory Game

Rules Rap

Functional Print Books

The Rules Book (page 25) is one example of a functional print book that can be used to help children understand the importance of reading and writing. Other classroom books that can help children with print connections include a Tooth Book to record the big event of losing their teeth or a Boo Boo Book to record the little scrapes and scratches children receive and to help them feel better.

Kiss Your Brain!

On the front of a ruled notebook, write *Kiss Your Brain!* Use the notebook as a form of praise for students who learn new skills, answer questions creatively, or solve a classroom problem. Invite these students to sign the book and write about what they did to receive this privilege.

Why

The catchy beat and words to this song will reinforce classroom rules and encourage positive behavior. The expectations are simple and positive, and the book can be used on a daily basis.

What

THE RULES RAP DANCE

Help children learn the words and internalize the rules by teaching them the following actions to *Rules Rap*.

The rules, the rules, the rules of the classroom.
(Snap fingers as you sway back and forth to the beat.)

Follow, follow, follow directions,
(Point index fingers in the air.)

Feet and hands, feet and hands,
(Point to feet and then each hand.)

Small voices inside, tall voices on the playground.
(Put finger over lips and then point out the window.)

Take care of your things, and keep the classroom neat and clean.
(Brush palms together to the beat.)

Work together, get along, and respect each other.
(Clasp hands together and then make circular motions like you're stirring a pot.)

RULES BOOK

Discuss with your students why rules are important, and encourage them to think about what would happen if there were no rules. Give each child a copy of page 26, and ask him or her to draw a picture of a rule that he or she thinks is important. Have the child dictate the rule or write it below the picture. Use book rings to bind all of the pictures together to make a class book. Hang the book in a prominent place in your classroom. When a child is behaving inappropriately, get out the book and find a page that relates to the behavior. Show it to the child as you say, *The book says you need to* (rule).

LUCKY STICKS

This idea will ensure that every child in your room gets a turn to be your special helper. Pass out jumbo craft sticks to the children, and ask them to write their names on the sticks and decorate them. Place all of the sticks in a can or cup labeled *Lucky Sticks*. When there is a special job to be done, pull a lucky stick from the can. After that child has had a turn, place his or her stick in an envelope in your desk. Continue until all of the sticks have been drawn and every child has had a turn.

Message for the Teacher

On the front of a spiral notebook, write *Things the Teacher Needs to Know*. Explain to your students that you won't always have time to listen to all the things they want to tell you during the day, but if they write their concerns down in the message book, you will look at them later. When children come to you to complain or tattle, hand them the book and say, *Write it all down, and don't leave out a thing!*

Lucky Tickets

Copy the tickets on page 27. Cut them apart and place them in a paper bag. Let children who exemplify behaviors in the *Rules Rap* choose a ticket. They may keep their tickets and redeem them whenever they want. Choose the lucky ticket incentives that match the abilities and interests of your students.

Name _____   Date _____

Our Class Rules

Draw a picture that tells about a good class rule. Write the rule on the lines below.

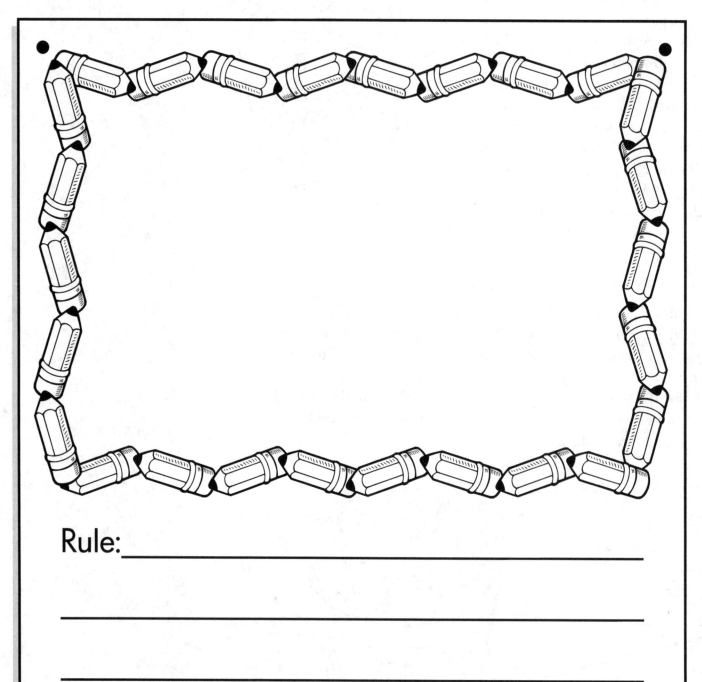

Rule:_____

_____

_____

_____

_____

Sing Along & Read Along with Dr. Jean Resource Guide © 2008 Creative Teaching Press

Lucky Tickets

Choose a book for story time.	Choose a song to sing.	Choose a game to play outside.
Be line leader.	Sit next to the teacher.	Sit next to a favorite friend for a day.
Read a book with a friend.	Listen to a story.	Do a job for your teacher.
Make something at the art center.	Play a computer game.	Write on the white board.
Sit at the teacher's desk.	Take a classroom game home for a night.	15 minutes free time to do whatever you want in the classroom.
Have the teacher call your parents to tell them what a great kid you are!	Choose an indoor game for the class to play.	Visit the library for 15 minutes.
Play a board game of your choice with a friend.	Create a puppet out of a paper bag.	Find a friend and draw a picture together.

Birdies

Animal Families

Divide the class into two groups. One group will be the parents and the other group will be the babies. Whisper the name of an animal in each "parent's" ear. Whisper the same animal names in the babies' ear. When the teacher says, *Find your babies*, tell all animals to start making their sounds as they walk around the room. When children find the person making a similar sound, have them sit down together. After playing the game, read the poem on page 31 and ask the children to identify the sounds the animals make.

Why This book will allow children to explore the concept of mother and baby animals. It also introduces ways to talk about different styles of singing, reading, and talking.

What

LOUD AND SOFT

Share the book with the class. As they listen to the song, ask children to identify the pages where the song is loud. Then ask them why it is silly to shout *Don't wake the birdies!* Use other familiar nursery rhymes and poems and say or sing them in different ways. For example:

Slow and fast–Say very slowly and then quickly.

Like a monster–Say with a deep voice.

Like a mouse–Say with a high, squeaky voice.

With emotions–Say happy, sad, mad, or scared.

With a cold–Hold your nose.

Like a pirate–Talk out of the side of your mouth.

Like a rock star–Pretend to hold a guitar and dance.

BIRD WATCHERS

Have children make pretend binoculars for bird watching. First, help children cut paper towel tubes in half and tape the two halves together. Then punch a hole in the topside of each and tie on a piece of string so that children can easily slip the binoculars over their heads. Take children on a nature walk, and let them look for birds with their binoculars. When you return to the classroom, allow children to draw pictures using the reproducible on page 30 and then write stories about what they saw.

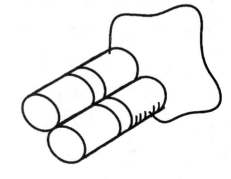

BIRDIE MOTIONS

Children will develop their gross motor skills and have the opportunity to practice their loud and soft tones acting out these movements to the story:

Way up in the sky the big birdies fly.
(Stretch out arms and flap them like wings.)

Way down in the nest the little birdies rest.
(Lay head on palms.)

With a wing on the left and a wing on the right,
(Tuck left hand in armpit and flap. Tuck right hand in armpit and flap.)

The little birdies sleep all through the night.
(Lay head on palms.)

SHHHHHHH!
(Put index finger over lips and whisper.)

DON'T WAKE UP THE BIRDIES!
(Cup hands around mouth and pretend to shout.)

Then up comes the sun.
(Make a circle over your head.)

The dew falls away.
(Bring palms down.)

Good morning! Good morning! the little birdies say.
(Throw hands up in the air each time you say good morning and smile.)

BIRD NEST

Model for children how to make a bird nest using a paper lunch bag. Begin by opening it up and rolling down from the top edge of the bag in an outward motion until you get to the bottom. It will now look like a little bird's nest. Make birds by cutting 7½" x 1¾" strips of light blue paper, one for each child.

Cut ¾" vertical slits two inches in from each end of the strip. Loop around the strip, insert and slide the slit ends together. Have students gently toss the loop into the air and watch it fly and twirl like a bird. Then have the children place their birds in their paper bag nests to rest.

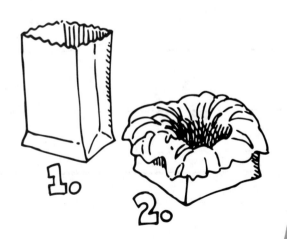

Dramatize

Choose three children to be baby birds, and choose one child to be the mother bird. Have the baby birds pretend to sleep as the mother bird flies around them. Then have the baby birds jump up at the appropriate time and say, *Good morning! Good morning!*

Same and Different

Begin a discussion about birds by asking students, *How are the birds in the book alike? How are they different?* and *How are all birds alike?* Record children's thoughts and ideas by using a Venn diagram. Then allow students to share what they know about birds or ask questions that they may have.

Bird Watching

Draw a picture of what you saw on your bird watch. Then write about your picture.

I saw...

_____

_____

_____

_____

Sing Along & Read Along with Dr. Jean Resource Guide © 2008 Creative Teaching Press

Animal Families

The father is a bull.
The mother is a cow.
The baby is a calf.
It wants some milk right now.

The father is a gander.
The mother is a goose.
The baby is a gosling.
It says "honk! honk!" to you!

The mother pig's a sow.
The father is a boar.
The baby is a piglet.
It eats and eats some more!

The father is a lion,
The mother a lioness.
The baby is a cub
And always in a mess!

The father horse is a stallion.
The mother is a mare.
The baby is a colt
And wobbles everywhere!

The father is a rooster.
The mother is a hen.
The babies are called chicks.
They peep and peep again!

The mother goat's a Nanny.
Billy's the father, it's true.
The babies are called kids—
And people have kids, too!

Animals have families,
Just like you and me.
Some are large and some are
small—they're special as can be!

–Dr. Holly Karapetkova

Nursery Rhyme Rally

Why Phonological awareness is essential to beginning reading and a foundation for literacy that all chilldren need. This book will entertain children while building skills with rhyme, rhythm, and alliteration.

What

BRAIN EXERCISE

Think of an imaginary line right down the middle of your body from your head to your toes. That's called your midline. Every time children cross over that line, they are exercising their brains by building "bridges" or connections between the two hemispheres. Have children cross their left hands to their right knees and then their right hands to their left knee, as they sing *Nursery Rhyme Rally*.

Try these dance motions to excerise the brain!

Disco –Stick your right finger in the air and then bring it down in front of you to your left side.

Swim –Move your arms in a swimming motion, crossing arms one at a time in front of your body.

Washing Machine –Hold your fists together and move them in a circle in front of your body.

Twist –Bend back and forth from your waist in time with the beat.

Apple Picking –Take your right arm and reach left as you pretend to pick an apple. Then take left arm and pretend to pick an apple on the right.

Windmill –Stand up tall and then bend your right hand down to touch your left foot. Stand up tall again and bend your left hand down to touch your right foot.

Patty–Cake –Get a partner and play patty–cake to the beat. Clap hands and then cross and tap right hands with your partner. Clap hands and cross and tap left hands with your partner.

Dramatizations

Let children act out different nursery rhymes. Choose characters for each rhyme, and let the children create their own movements. You could also play a game similar to charades in which a child acts out a rhyme as classmates try to guess the character.

Who? Where? Why?

Use nursery rhymes to begin talking about story elements. Look through the book and have children identify the characters in each rhyme. Ask questions such as *Where is the setting?* and *What is the problem?*

NURSERY RHYME JUKEBOX

To make "CDs" for the jukebox, begin by cutting six 5" circles out of poster board. Copy page 34. Color the CD labels and cut them out. Glue them to the poster board circles. Place the CDs in a gift bag, and write *Jukebox* on the front. When you have a few extra minutes, choose a child to reach in the jukebox and pull out a rhyme for the class to repeat. Add additional CDs to the jukebox as your students learn new rhymes.

NURSERY RHYME CLUB

Create a poster that says *Nursery Rhyme Club*. Make copies of the membership cards on page 35. When a child can stand in front of the room and repeat a nursery rhyme, he or she can join the Nursery Rhyme Club. Let children sign their names on the poster, and give them their membership cards.

Transition Tune

Use the tune of "100 Bottles of Pop on the Wall" for singing other nursery rhymes during transitions, such as cleaning up or washing hands. You can also sing most of the nursery rhymes to the tune of "Yankee Doodle."

Rhyming Words

Have children listen to each nursery rhyme and identify the words that rhyme. Write these words on the board. Have children circle letters that are the same in each set of words. Challenge the children to think of other words that rhyme.

Nursery Rhyme Jukebox

Jack and Jill

Little Boy Blue

Hickory
Dickory
Dock

Little Miss Muffet

Mary, Mary,
Quite Contrary

Old Mother
Hubbard

Nursery Rhyme Club

Nursery Rhyme Club

_____
Name

is an official member for reciting
a nursery rhyme!

Nursery Rhyme Club

_____
Name

is an official member for reciting
a nursery rhyme!

Nursery Rhyme Club

_____
Name

is an official member for reciting
a nursery rhyme!

Nursery Rhyme Club

_____
Name

is an official member for reciting
a nursery rhyme!

Nursery Rhyme Club

_____
Name
is an official member for reciting
a nursery rhyme!

Nursery Rhyme Club

_____
Name
is an official member for reciting
a nursery rhyme!

End on a Positive Note

Sing this song to end your day in a positive way. Have children hold hands and stand in a circle. At the end of the song, ask children to say something they did that made them feel proud or have them pay a compliment to a friend.

Things to Be Happy About

Make a class big book called Things to Be Happy About. Give each child a sheet of large white construction paper (12" x 18"). Ask children to draw things that make them happy. Encourage children to label their pictures or dictate their ideas to an adult. Add construction paper covers and include a sheet for the title page. Glue a picture of each child on the title page and decorate the front cover by having children write their names and draw smiley faces. Bind the pages together and place the book in your classroom library.

May There Always Be Sunshine

Why As children sing along with this book, they will learn how to cooperate and that it is important to stick together and help each other.

What

STICK PUPPETS

Have children color the faces on page 38, cut them out, and glue them to jumbo craft sticks. Invite children to hold up their puppets as they share what makes them happy, sad, angry, or scared. Ask children what they can do when they feel that way. Hold up puppets as you sing these different verses to the tune of "If You're Happy and You Know It."

 | If you're happy and you know it, give a smile
If you're sad and you know it, rub your eyes
If you're angry and you know it, stomp your feet
If you're scared and you know it, shiver and shake

MOVEMENT WANDS

Staple several strips of tissue paper cut 24" x 2" to a straw. Have children wave the wands as they sing "May There Always Be Sunshine" and other songs.

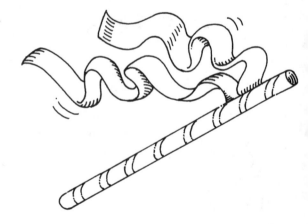

SIGN LANGUAGE

Teach children the manual signs for key words in the song so they can "sing" with their hands.

 May there always be–Index finger points up and rotates clockwise away from the body.

Sunshine–Make a circle with the index finger above the head and then turn the hand toward the head with the fingers spread out like the sun.

Blue–Make "b" with hand and pivot at wrist.

Sky–Hand moves in an arc over head to indicate sky.

Children–Palm turned as if resting on a child's head.

You–Point to friend.

Story–Make circles with thumbs and index fingers of both hands and touch the circles together several times.

Music–Extend arm and pretend to strum with palm of other hand.

Teacher–Fingertips at temples, pull out and then open and come down.

Care–Make "k" with both hands and cross wrists.

*Visit aslpro.com for clarification of signs.

MY SCHOOL

Ask children to look at the illustrations in the book and describe how the school in the pictures is like their school. Then ask children how their school is different. Sing the following song to the tune of "The Wheels on the Bus" to help children learn the name of their school, teacher, principal, city, and state.

 The name of my school is (<u>name of your school</u>),
(<u>Name of your school</u>), (<u>name of your school</u>).
The name of my school is (<u>name of your school</u>).
That's the name of my school.

Feelings

Ask children how sunny days make them feel. Have children share about happy times. Ask children how cloudy days make them feel. Have children talk about days that have not gone well for them. Explain to children that every day we have new experiences and different feelings. And that's OK. Brainstorm with the class different feelings children experience. Give students copies of page 39. Ask them to draw pictures to represent different feelings they may have.

Feelings Puppets

Name _____   Date _____

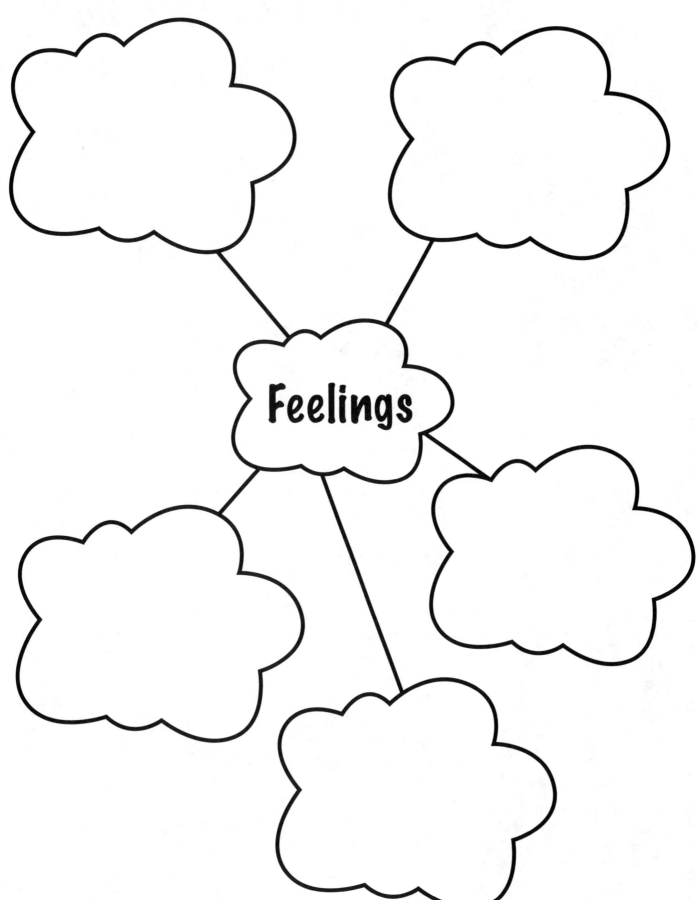

Feelings

Eating Number Sets

Give each child a divided paper plate (the ones shaped like animals are really fun) and a handful of cereal. Demonstrate how to make sets in the smaller sections. Bring the sets together in the larger section and count how many in all.

Food Numerals

Call children's attention to the illustrations on each page. Ask how the illustrator turned the food into a numeral. Invite students to trace over the numerals with their fingers or a pointer.

Hint: This is a good time to discuss the different ways to write numerals such as 4 and 9. Use the computer to demonstrate different fonts and show children how numerals and letters can vary.

Why This book will help children learn numerals, number words, and counting forwards. The rhyme, rhythm, and silliness are always appealing to children.

What

OLD LADY PUPPET

Children will be delighted to use their own "old lady" prop with the story. Have them color and cut out the head, hands, and feet on page 42. Help children glue the hands and feet to 6" x 1" strips of paper and staple them to the side of a resealable plastic bag as shown. Staple the head to the back opening of the bag. Have children cut out the numbers at the bottom and insert them in the old lady's tummy as they read or sing along with the book.

NUMBER STORIES

Introduce children to word problems with simple stories using the old lady. For example, *If the old lady eats one apple and three oranges, how many things has she eaten in all?* Have students write their own number stories on the reproducible on page 43.

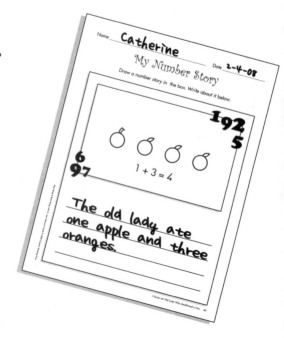

PLAY DOUGH NUMERALS

Purchase play dough or make your own play dough from the recipe below. Take plastic plates or place mats and write a different numeral on each one with a permanent marker. Demonstrate how to make play dough numerals by rolling the dough into snakes and placing them on top of the numerals. Ask children to do this for each numeral.

Homemade Play Dough

2 cups flour

2 cups salt

2 tablespoons cream of tartar

2 tablespoons vegetable oil

2 cups water

1 of each: red, blue, yellow food coloring

Mix ingredients together in a pan until smooth. Cook over medium heat, stirring constantly until the mixture forms a ball and sticks to the spoon. Cool and knead. Store in a resealable plastic bag.

*Substitute the vegetable oil with baby oil, or aroma therapy oil to add a different scent. Or for other aromas try adding unsweetened Kool-Aid, vanilla, cinnamon, or other spices to the play dough.

Invisible Writing

Have children extend one arm in the air and pretend to write the numbers with their index fingers as you sing each page in the book.

Palm Pilots

Have children practice writing numbers, shapes, and letters on their "palm pilots." Ask children to hold up the palm of one hand and trace numbers on their palm with the index finger of the other hand.

I Know an Old Lady
Who Swallowed a One

1	2	3	4	5
6	7	8	9	10

Sing Along & Read Along with Dr. Jean Resource Guide © 2008 Creative Teaching Press

Name _____ Date _____

My Number Story

Draw a number story in the box. Write about it below.

_____

_____

_____

_____

Thumb Kiss

Acknowledge a job well done or good behavior by going up to each child and giving him or her a "thumb kiss." Extend your thumb and touch it to the child's thumb as you make a smacking sound with your lips in praise of his or her efforts and achievements.

Pat on the Back

Trace around children's hands and let them cut the tracings out. Write a positive comment about each child on his or her hand cut out. Tape the hands to the children's backs to wear home at the end of the day.

Twinkle Friends

Why

Jump-start your day with a song like "Twinkle Friends" and set a positive tone that will excite children's brains and make them feel good. By supporting feelings of worthiness, children will develop a sensitivity toward others.

What

TWINKLE FRIENDS DANCE

Have children find a partner and make the following motions as they sing:

Twinkle, twinkle little me.
(Extend arms in air and gently touch fingertips with partner.)
I'm as special as can be.
(Point to self with thumb.)
There's no one quite like me, it's true,
(Shake head no.)
And my friends are special, too.
(Point to partner.)
Twinkle, twinkle little me,
(Touch fingertips in air with partner.)
I'm as special as can be.
(Point to self with thumb.)
Twinkle, twinkle, little star,
(Touch fingertips in air with partner.)
What a special friend you are.
(Point to friend.)
From your head to your toes,
(Point to partner's head, then feet.)
We are special friends, you know.
(Grasp hands with partner and swing around.)
Twinkle, twinkle, little star,
(Touch fingertips in air with partner.)
What a special friend you are.
(Hug partner.)

Continue singing the song as children move around the room and find new partners.

KINDNESS TICKETS

Discuss what it means to be a friend. Use a word web to write down words children suggest about friends. Reproduce and cut apart the "kindness tickets" on page 46. Encourage children to give a kindness ticket to friends when they see them doing something kind.

MAGIC MIRROR

Glue a small mirror in the bottom of a shoebox. Explain to the children that the most wonderful thing in the world is in the box. It's so special that there's only one like it in the whole world. Pass the box around and watch children's smiles as they lift the lid and see themselves!

SPECIAL ME

Have children illustrate something special about themselves on the reproducible on page 47. Then invite them to make "Special Me" badges using the pattern at the bottom of page 47. Have students color and cut out the badges. Pin the badges on the children as they share their illustrations and tell about what makes themselves special.

Buddy Sticks

Learning with a friend is an effective way for children to scaffold knowledge to a higher level. Make Buddy Sticks to ensure children interact with a variety of partners. You will need a jumbo craft stick for each child in the class. Put identical stickers at the ends of every two sticks. If you have an odd number of students, make an additional stick for partnering with the teacher or make one group of three. Place all of the sticks sticker-side down in a can labeled *Buddy Sticks*. When it is time for children to work with a buddy, have them draw sticks to find their partners.

Kindness Tickets

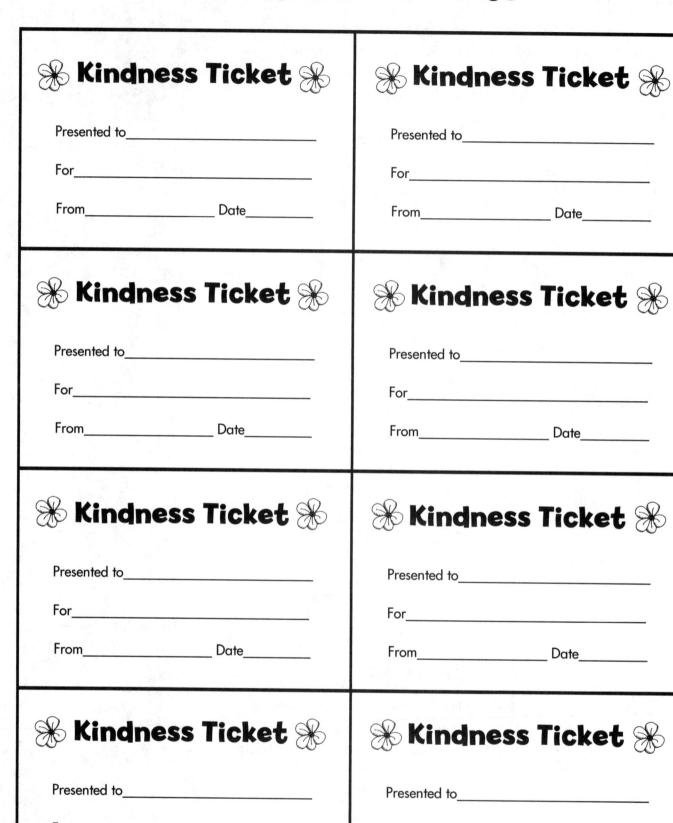

❀ **Kindness Ticket** ❀

Presented to_____

For_____

From_____ Date_____

❀ **Kindness Ticket** ❀

Presented to_____

For_____

From_____ Date_____

❀ **Kindness Ticket** ❀

Presented to_____

For_____

From_____ Date_____

❀ **Kindness Ticket** ❀

Presented to_____

For_____

From_____ Date_____

❀ **Kindness Ticket** ❀

Presented to_____

For_____

From_____ Date_____

❀ **Kindness Ticket** ❀

Presented to_____

For_____

From_____ Date_____

❀ **Kindness Ticket** ❀

Presented to_____

For_____

From_____ Date_____

❀ **Kindness Ticket** ❀

Presented to_____

For_____

From_____ Date_____

Sing Along & Read Along with Dr. Jean Resource Guide © 2008 Creative Teaching Press

Name _____   Date _____

Cartoons

Draw speech bubbles on the board, and explain how cartoonists use these to show readers what the characters are saying. Have children help you name characters in the book and tell the sounds that they make. Write the sounds in the speech bubbles on the board. Then provide paper and invite children to draw pictures of themselves "talking" in speech bubbles.

Families

Ask children to share what they think a family is. Discuss how families are alike and how they are different. Make a class graph of the number of people in each child's family. Then have students make a family map using the reproducible on page 50.

My Mother Is a Baker

Why Children will develop auditory memory, oral language, gross motor skills, and sequencing skills as they read and sing about this cartoon family. The book will also serve as a springboard for children to talk about families and occupations.

What

FAMILY MOVES

Teach children how to make the following motions for the different characters in the song:

Mother–Pat tummy as you say, "Yum! Yum!"

Father–Pretend to drive a car as you say, "Vroom! Vroom!"

Sister–Extend arms above your head as you say, "La ta de da, and a toodly doo!"

Brother–Pretend to twirl a lasso as you say, "Yahoo!"

Doggie–Tilt your head back as you bark, "Woof! Woof!"

Kitty–Pretend to pet your arm as if a cat were in your arms, "Purr! Purr!"

Baby–Shake fists and open mouth wide as you "WAH!"

WHAT COMES NEXT?

After reading the story with the class, ask students to name the characters in the order they appear, and write them on the board. Ask the children to identify who was first, second, third, and so forth. Give each child a sentence strip and a copy of the reproducible on page 51. Help children fold their sentence strips into eighths, and then open and fold the strip back and forth like an accordion. Next, ask children to cut out the title and character cards. Help children lay the cards in sequential order begining with the title and glue them into place on their sentence strips. Invite children to use the books they made to point to the characters as they sing along with the story.

MY HOUSE

Use the directions below to fold a piece of paper into the shape of a house. Write a child's name and address on the front of each house. Have children draw a picture of their families on the inside of the house.

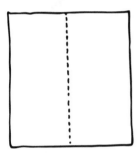 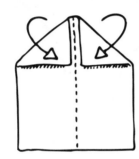 

1. Fold in half lengthwise.

2. Bring in corners to the middle fold to make the roof.

3. Fold up the bottom edge of the paper and line that edge up to the bottom edge of the roof to make the body of the house.

WHAT DO YOU DO?

Have children interview their parents to find out about their jobs. Generate a list of questions for the children to ask parents. For example:

1. How did you learn to do your job?
2. Do you use math in your job?
3. Do you read and write in your job?
4. Do you wear special clothing for your job?
5. What do you like best about your job?

Then have the children draw and write about what they learned. Invite children to share their findings with the class.

Many Homes

Ask children to think about different places in which families can live. Take students to the library, and look for books that show different places where people live. Have children draw pictures of the different places and types of homes they find. Help children label their pictures.

Pet Parade

Ask children to bring in photographs of their pets for a pet parade. Invite small groups of children to describe their pets and then walk around the room holding their pictures. After the parade, allow children to draw pictures of their pets. Then cut the front and back off a box of dog biscuits. Put the children's artwork between the two box panels, hole-punch, and bind with book rings to make a class pet book.

Hint: If children don't have a pet, ask them to draw a picture of a pet they would like to have.

My Family

My Mother Is a Baker

My Mother Is a Baker	**Brother** — Yahoo!
Mother — Yum! Yum!	**Doggie** — Woof! Woof!
Father — Vroom! Vroom!	**Kitty** — Purr! Purr!
Sister — La ta de da, and a toodly doo!	**Baby** — WAH!

Simon Says

Play a game of "Simon Says" in which you refer to the body parts in Spanish. For example, *Simon says put your hands on your cabeza. Simon says touch your orejas.*

Handprint Art

Trace around children's hands and feet on construction paper. Have children cut out these shapes and glue them to a different sheet of paper to create animals and other objects.

Why The younger children are when they are introduced to a second language, the more successful they will be in learning it. This book is a natural way to introduce Spanish words for common body parts.

What ## BODY PARTS

Engaging students' gross motor skills and connecting physical movements with words will help students remember the names of the body parts in English and in Spanish. Have children point to their own body parts as you sing this song.

Then give children the body outline on page 54. Have them fill in the outline with their own faces and features. Read over the labels at the bottom of the page with the children. Then have them cut out the labels and glue them to their pictures near the correct body parts and draw lines to match.

BODY PARTS COUNTING

Ask, *How many mouths do you have? Ears? Fingers? Toes?* Have the children count along by ones for the number of mouths in the room or by twos for the number of ears in the room. Have each child hold up one hand and count by fives for the number of fingers. For fun, count toes by tens.

THE FIVE SENSES

Ask, *What do you use your eyes for? Ears? Nose? Mouth? Hands?* Teach children the song below about the five senses. Sing it to the tune of "BINGO." Discuss the five senses with the class. Have students share about some of the senses they use throughout their day. Then have children make their own My Five Senses books using the reproducible on page 55. Have children complete each sentence draw matching pictures and cut the strips apart. Help children staple the pages on the left-hand side.

Five Senses

I have five senses that I use

To help me learn each day.

See, hear, smell, taste, touch.

See, hear, smell, taste, touch.

See, hear, smell, taste, touch

I use them every day.

My Five Senses

Name Carrie   Date 3/18/08

I can smell flowers.

I can hear music.

I can taste pizza.

I can see colors.

I can touch my dog.

My Hands on My Head 55

Parent Talk

Ask children in your classroom if they know any other languages. For homework have children ask their parents if they know another language. If they do, have the children ask their parents to teach them how to say *hello* in that language. Make a poster with all the different ways to say *hello*.

Gracias!

Teach children how to say *please, thank you,* and other common phrases in Spanish and repeat these words throughout the day.

Please – por favor
Thank you – gracias
Friend – amigo
Girl – chica
Boy – chico
Hello – hola
Good-bye – adios
Good – bueno
How are you? – ¿Como esta usted?
Very well – Muy bien

Mi nombre es_____.

cabeza head	orejas ears	ojos eyes	nariz nose	boca mouth	panza tummy	pies feet

Sing Along & Read Along with Dr. Jean Resource Guide © 2008 Creative Teaching Press

My Five Senses

I can smell _____.

I can hear _____.

I can taste _____.

I can see _____.

I can touch _____.

Notes